OTHER
WORLDS,
IN
OTHER
WORDS

OTHER WORLDS, IN OTHER WORDS

- poems -

JERRY LOVELADY

atmosphere press

For my mother, Jeanette who, on her death bed, thought I stole all of her poems. She worked hard her entire life to raise six children and set aside her own aspirations for our welfare. Greatest thanks to her for teaching me how to be patient with myself and inspiring me to write poetry.

Author's Note

This book is my second undertaking. *Other Worlds, In Other Words* is a compilation of poems I describe as eclectic in nature. I don't try to severely separate past times and lives with the present one. No one knows the true make up of reality. Most of us believe that we are living only right here, right now, from all the observations that we can make for ourselves. I choose to deem all viewpoints correct, as the observer presents them. All philosophical and political disputes may be settled by the combatants at a later date.

I prefer to write surrealistic poetry that accentuates the everyday, mundane happenings in our lives such as the effects of changing weather outside, how we observe darkness and light interacting, and the awesome power and mystery of Nature and man's place in it. I also like to think about how the ancients viewed their world and how that compares to what we see and feel about the same occurrences in present times.

Here are four short sections of poems about the ways people spend their leisure moments remembering other times and worlds they lived in, their psychological frame of mind while living in them, and their spiritual condition as it progressed from there, or may be progressing as they live their lives now.

I have also included some poems about how we handle our romantic lives, our other personal relationships and some allegorical observations of Nature and humankind interacting poorly, or not, touching on the innocence of youth, our decisions when we were younger and how they affect us when we are older.

I like to believe that it is reality's nature to limit our perceptions in order to operate unobserved at other levels. It is not in our own nature to observe things in a multi-faced manner. By presenting itself to us in this way, Nature forces us to slow down our observation of events, analyze them thoroughly for flaws and draw our own conclusions. Coincidentally, this is also how good science works best, applied in this empirical manner. Are our conclusions always correct or just guesses about the nature of reality? No one knows.

When several people observe the same event, happening at the same time in the same place, they often derive differing conclusions about that event. Most are similar, but their descriptions may vary widely from one individual to the next. This difference in perspectives fascinates me, so much so that many of my poems are concerned with our perceptions, particularly in the realm of natural phenomena.

Other Worlds, In Other Words treats all of these observations as real events, unfolding them just enough to allow the reader to decide both what is existential and what may be occurring at other levels of reality.

If other worlds do exist, they must surely flourish most vividly in our creative, analytical minds. As any scientist worth their salt will tell you, science is an objective approach to extremely subjective phenomena. Anything can and may happen.

For instance, in the field of quantum physics it has been discovered that the act of observing certain sub-atomic particles may cause them to behave differently than when they are not being observed. Subjected to careful observation, electrons begin to behave like waves rather than particles. Under the right conditions electrons can also exist in more than one place at the same time. This could mean that there are indeed other existences separated only by time and a little space in between them, coexisting right under our noses. If anyone is a science denier, it might be fair to say that, under the right conditions, our observations may not actually line up with reality.

It is no small wonder that our ancestors were so superstitious. Explanations of how crops grew, why the seasons changed, how the tides worked, even human and animal conception of their offspring must have baffled them. With very few observable clues from which to draw conclusions they relied on mystical explanations for most everyday events they encountered. In modern times we see interest in mysticism resurfacing, along with a rejection of scientific explanations for our physical world. Probably one of the most drastic is the "Flat Earth Movement". Without getting too far into that particular subject, it is clear that some in our culture are seeking alternative explanations for what they see and hear as it pertains to the natural world. This spark of interest is very evident in modern societies and noteworthy, whatever other factors may be contributing believable evidence explaining these phenomena.

Meanings for all that we sense are derived from conclusions that, in turn, are drawn from analyzing our observations. We usually fail to recognize or appreciate what we casually encounter around us. The pace of life is so advanced we rarely find the time to think about what we see and acknowledge as real on a daily basis. Acknowledged or not, these events may have great bearing on our lives. I do not believe that some of the things I describe here really exist, but it is pleasant to imagine that they do. Who really knows?

I think fate, destiny, Karma, God's will, whatever you want to call it, perhaps all of them, play parts in my life each day, so I try to live the best life that I can, being here and now.

I hope that you enjoy reading my book and that you will share it with your friends.

"What happens tomorrow is already done. I am just hanging around to see what part I am playing."

Jerry Lovelady

2-9-1993

Table of Contents

Part Three: Love Builds Its Own Universe

Part Four: Homespun World Views and Alternate Histories

Part One

The Was, That Is Me
No More

Wreckage of My Zombie Past

The wreckage of my zombie past catches up with me again
like the palace grounds at Versailles carelessly sullied by tourists'
debris.
Broken lives spawn countless un-kept promises.
They badger me with their relentless ruckus.
What I thought to be abandoned for good
now triggers the trip wire alarm.
Again Zombie misdeeds patrol the byways of my brain.
Old bones were carelessly tossed
into the closet of forgetfulness.
The door I savagely slammed shut
is now thrown open for all
to gawk at and judge.
A graveyard of perennially bad ideas,
lifeless, hollow dreams piled up there moldering.
Some struggle to rise with deafening
clinking and clacking in my frightened ears.

Graveyards full of ideas prematurely perished, some buried alive,
many others stillborn or aborted.
All were unremarkably expired ideas,
randomly forgotten detritus of disasters.
Hastily exhumed and reanimated
they find new legs, marauding as they roam about.
They refuse to lie in repose,
eager to tromp about unimpeded.
The trash bin of time overflows
with the wastes of the past.
Useless wrapping papers joy ride down my inner freeways,
haphazardly hopscotching, riding on the draughts of passing traffic.
Stagnant breaths of congenital blight
mar an otherwise pristine mental landscape.
Sick thoughts and shabby deeds are conjured up
along with all the wastes of youthful talent.

Coughed up and wriggling come the lame,
unfulfilled promises and shabby un-divulged secrets.

Rattling bones flee like stirred up midges,
scattering in every direction.
Obtrusive and obvious,
these distractions abruptly alight, imposing themselves
on my otherwise mundane life.
Unwelcome messes proliferate wherever they land.

Like unannounced visitors they arrive,
unexpected and unwelcome,
from past lives most desirably
left forgotten.

The Was, That Is Me No More

Lax now lie once steely limbs with vise-like grip.
The cast iron stomach, overhung by an
I-beam straight back, now bent and bowed
beneath the weight of a new, frightening reality
that has made me bondservant to all its requirements.
Mighty Atlas stumbles beneath the staggering volume of
preconditions,
dubious plans proposed and demands to be met,
with dire consequences his reward for failure.
Gone is precious freedom to be alone with my thoughts.
Age strips away all pride as degradation follows
closely behind watching, waiting.
The judgment of a crueler world than I knew before
impatiently licks its slobbering jaws, ready to
snap me up without provocation or conscience.

A callous world holds no regard for antecedent values of
archaic lives lived or times cherished.
Into the forgetful past I am ultimately relegated,
not at peace and unhappy.
The leavings of me struggle to lie down, alone,
decrepit and impaired.
No more brag left in me, but how my bones complain.
If life were fair we'd live it backwards,
knowing right from wrong innately,
with no regrets, no more unforeseen circumstances.

Day by day the future unreeling frames of the past,
like a ribbon of dreams gently fluttering behind.
Life would be lived ever gently rolling backward
to a certain fresh beginning, away from the violent,
impassionate end all mortals fear.
Like a chrysalis, I would seek a new beginning
in a metamorphosis back to its egg, resulting in

new conclusions for every culmination of life's events,
far, all in all, the better for my toils.

No Boundaries

Open up his grave, that sod encrusted tomb.
A madman is buried at the bottom of the hole.
He wants to escape: his ideas are already
skewing precious reason, twisting minds
and provoking thoughts to rail against
a blatantly patent world which
he refused to fully inhabit till the half-life of never,
till the skies have fallen down.

Peel back the cool, moist earth.
Wake the worms that lunched on his earlobes;
let them sing his praises.
Strike the tombstone marker with new runes.
Brush the moss off of his name,
carve a tribute to his wisdom.
His words were a salve the world could use,
abruptly lost in the scramble for power.
Pick up an axe and chop at the wise roots
that search deeply to consume his bones.

Let him out: let him rise like vapor,
a fogbank of restless thoughts.
Let every disarticulated jaw bone
in the cemetery parrot his preaching.
Dust off his old bowler.
Place it on his crusty skull.
Clinking digits gesticulated wildly
when he spoke: they rattle unbearably now.
Just a wasted bag of bones remains to
inhabit his moldy coffin.
His ideas find no limits to their assent,
no boundaries on Earth, or above
can prevent their unearthing.

See him stand and boldly swagger forth.
A marauding giant to the timid men safely hidden
behind their castle walls quaking,
standing on one another's shoulders to steal a peek
at enlightened perfection resurrected, vindicated.
Death cannot triumph over greatness,
whether recognized or forgotten.

The Curious Cat

Panic made me flee from the church house
like a cockroach crawling out of the woodpile,
just before a fire is lit.
She almost had me.
I helplessly stumbled forward.
surreptitiously led to the altar
like any other unwilling sacrifice.

The gleam in her eyes frightened me.
Her face radiated a curious glow
as she tightened the tether
around my throat: I gulped.
She called me her pet.
She carried the quirt in a well-practiced manner.
The gold ring she gave me began to burn my finger.

I was blinded by the brilliance
of our nuptial fantasies.
We confounded those who saw us together.
They remarked that we made a dazzling couple.
We were inseparable idiots.
Disbelief, then approval they lavished upon us.

Our augurs predicted a rosy outcome.
A moment of clarity struck one day.
I had eagerly watched as my dream came to fruition.
The dream she wanted vanished like morning dew.
That day I realized I did not belong in her dream.
She only pretended to include me in her plans.
I could not pretend that things would stay the same,
that I could still be that other someone she wanted me to be.
I had to have all of her or nothing.
My get away was stealthy and swift.

Quietly I crawled back out of her life.
Months later, while I was still making my escape,
an accidental encounter brought us together again,
and for a brief interlude I imagined a new life
in which we might both be happy once more.
She talked softly as she pulled the blindfold
out of her overnight bag.
I did not feel a thing as she slipped it over my eyes.
We turned off into another dead end alley.

There I came face to face with a curious cat.
She eagerly played with me like I was a ball of yarn,
unraveling the loops, one by one, stretching me out.
Then suddenly, she turned away.
Not a whine or a mew did she utter.
She threw her tail in the air, and
without looking back, calmly walked
out of my life forever.

Sitting at Her Mirror (1)

Sitting at her mirror just the other day
she spied a wrinkle which only she
would have noticed, it was so tiny.
Will you still love me when I am old, she asked.

Your satin skin may not stay the same,
but a crevice or two, or twenty
could not change the way I feel about you.
Our love will only improve.

Another grey hair had found its way
to the crest of her long brown locks.
Her face showed disappointment and she remarked,
Seems like there is a new one every day.

She did not see the gleam in my eyes
as the light played upon her shapely silhouette.
Splendid silvery threads glinted softly as she sat.
How wealthy a man I am, I thought.

She stepped on the bathroom scale.
Her brow crinkled into a worried frown.
Still not as light as I had hoped to be, she retorted.
You are everything I had hoped for and more, I said.

Lovers and Fools

My tears are real,
clear and salty.
They choke my throat shut
as I try to swallow another
poor excuse I made up to explain why
my eyes are red and tired.
But, really it's because I had them
pinched shut too long
trying to hold back the sobs.

The page is getting wet.
My pen does not want to write this.
Something has gone terribly wrong here.
I never act this way.
Self-pity is the drunkenness of fools.
I am drunk and still hung over
from staying up late trying
to figure out why
I am not with you anymore.

This is not how the story
was supposed to end.
I should just let you go.
But, I can't just cut my arm off
trying to get away from someone
I feel attached to so permanently.
On the other hand,
maybe a chain saw...?

His Lessons in Love (2)

He could not really love another
until someone showed him how.
The ragged beggar saw his bleak image
in the fractured window panes of his tenement life.
He had become a stranger to himself.
Repulsed by his reflection, he abdicated responsibility
for the parts he played in the mad illusion, miming his roles
in a charade with no clues, no hints.
He finally understood the problem.
With determination, he uncorked the bottle
and poured out all his sorrows,
along with every conceivable form of self-punishment.

He had gotten a raw deal from everyone.
He stood utterly alone on an empty stage stammering out his lines.
He had written his life like a tragic play
with only himself cast to portray
the roles of all the characters;
the wicked criminal, the angry policeman,
the incredulous judge, the jaded juror and the heartless jailer.
The only key to his cell door he kept hidden
deep inside his locked box heart, a useless,
rusting relic that endured the unfelt decades.

Many tried to love him
the best ways that they knew how.
First to fail were his absent caregivers,
busy working parents with a large brood to look after.
They fed and clothed their fat, spoiled brat.
Even with all their effort they still managed to
fall short of his expectations.

For most of his life real love was a movie poster,
pretty to look at behind a glass case
outside the theater, but untouchable.
No one was worth the risk and pain of trying.
His idea of a suitable companion never coalesced.
Never did anyone quite measure up, not even his hapless wife
who he cruelly put off marrying, then took hostage
for a few more dreadful years.
None seemed special enough to give his all.
He did not know what they needed from him.
His long despair began to dissolve his life.

A failed marriage and several
destructive relationships later,
when he was not looking for anyone to fix him,
someone special merrily skipped into his life.
With a Cheshire cat smile and a sparkle in her eye
she blinked, and all the lonely years were swept away
in an instant.

At last the sun rose on his dark nightmare.
They began living in a storybook dream for two.
Like a fragile water lily he gently grasped the hand of Isis.
They walked around their palace grounds and chortled at their luck.
Their plans were carried out with impeccable clarity.
What before had seemed impossible to do
was made pleasantly simple, satisfying.
The three thousand piece jigsaw puzzle fell together.

Tantalus grasped his apple.
All he dreamed of was obtainable.
With the stealth of a cat burglar she reached
through the bars of his heart and stole the rusty key.
She unlocked the creaking cell door with a wink.
Welcome home, was all she whispered.
They never looked back again.

14

My Destiny

I dreamed that my Destiny passed me by
a week ago, or a month ago, or a year or two.
Destiny rules all time it lightly touches.
Unbound, it adheres to no snuggly fitting interval.
My Destiny flew by me like a bullet, stealthy and sudden.
I could not see it, nor did it announce itself.
Just the slightest puff of air
that I felt on my cheek as it passed me by,
telling me that it had silently missed me
as I sat blissfully ignorant, totally unaware,
un-attentive, not a single clue,
that this was my Destiny
leaving me behind,
abandoning me to my own choices
forever.
But, forever is such a long time to risk being
without a Destiny to fall back on.
I now wait patiently for my Destiny
to come round the corner again
so that I may once more believe in something other
than my feeble self to get me by.

The Boy I Knew

The dashing ghost of the boy he thought he knew
still haunts the hollow halls of his hidden fortress,
stronghold of the ripe and rotting fruits he left behind
to sour with age, now just wasted memories and useless ideas.
Shrinking standup stature, drooping wrinkled pants,
razor thin profile, almost a shadow thick.
Flickering coals coalesce where
once brilliant flames had blazed.
Dazzling idol's stare, radiant smile,
mountain lakes mirrored skies of blue in crystal eyes.
A flash of grin rode atop
a streaking satyr's form.

He trotted by so fast, to catch a glimpse
of him was hard.
A sleekly streamlined engine leaving the station,
now left rusting and abandoned on the siding,
all its steam bled off so very long ago.
Caricatures of his past lives
creep tauntingly to and fro.
Children laugh at his creaking back, withered and bent.
His brittle limbs complain,
feebly gripping fingers crackle and pop.

This most precious place of myriad venial pleasures
comes complimentary with agonizing pains.
His redemption: to just fade away to nothing.
None would miss him and
quite few would dare complain if he was gone.
None can hold out hope to stop
the relentless process of decay.
Applaud it loudly or
lament in silent sorrow.

Better just to fade away and
cut his losses.
Sweet oblivion, served up
pure and undiluted.
No drug or drink affords
such solitude unending.
Escape he sought through all
those years in a younger body.
In better times, before
it got him all worn out.

Fleeting thoughts of final
solitude he once feared
hold some welcome kind
of intrigue for him now.
No regret for what he
ever did or did not do.
Time now for resting,
hard earned reprieve,
perhaps the end.

Beyond This Dream

He failed to achieve what they demanded.
Instead, he was compelled to be what he became.
The was, that is him no more,
frightened them and strengthened him.
His disparities made him whole.

Bury the crumpled creature you found lying there.
He will not protest how deep or shallow.
His meager life was a child's daydream at best.
His new life now flourishes in a different milieu,
that none could ever have prophesied.

Should you write his epitaph,
he requires neither name nor date upon the stone.
In the interim his bare feet will dance
lightly on the grass
to melodies not yet imagined or heard.

Being Here and Now

The events which trouble me most
do not really exist.
They are merely the anxious forebodings of a
tomorrow that has not yet happened.
Scraps of the past form clustered dramas, frightful flash mobs
renditions with inappropriate costume changes,
performed again, and again by distastefully familiar actors,
leaving blank spots in the script for the mind to fix upon
or discard.

There are stark reminders of the smoldering wreckage,
discarded junkyard lives demolished and forgotten,
soon misplaced by my forgetful conscience.
Neither the past nor the future holds any hope
for serenity.
Life for me is snuggly nestled in the present.
Nothing can wholly bother or disrupt an existence
in the here and now.

Though specters may cast long shadows
over my shoulder,
only a raw and certain,
raucous and lively today exists for me.
An honest today makes no promises,
hollow or unfulfilled.

The ever unfolding now rolls on.
Hand on shoulder, hour, follows glorious hour,
unreeling a series of totally unscripted
and novel events.
Previously unwitnessed and unlived,
no moment is born quite the same as another.

The children of an omnipresent God
revel in each day's uniqueness.
None have lived this day before.
The real or imagined events they encounter
are entirely owned and operated
by them.
No one may duplicate their day's
quiet freshness, or
its myriad complexities.

The child in me awakens and counts his heartbeats,
striving eagerly to wait for pleasures soon gathered.
Queued up at each new pathway I stand momentarily united
with my brethren, admiring each facet of a diamond's clarity,
found glittering in the newly forming day.
All this may only be fully appreciated
by being here and now.

Fairy Tales and Fantasies

Vaguely intrigued we carried on
like giddy teenaged burnouts.
The dream caught fire and collapsed
for both heroes and villains,
tragic conclusion to an applaudable farce.
We needed more than longing glances,
promising much, but meaning very little.
Wistful words whispered under your breath
when no one else was near
to hear them but me
were no better than silence,
worse than lies.

Your secrets kept you in chains,
so, you attempted to shackle us together.
You made discrete promises
we both knew you never meant to keep.
The sweet fantasies you ardently
wished for me to believe
fell apart over time, as we did.
In another life we might have made it work.
I guess you hoped to console me
panting out more half-baked untruths
about how great it was going to be, married.
Your well-practiced groans of ecstasy
on my rumpled sheets almost had me fooled.

You were my Eos and the dawn
always broke brightly when you smiled.
You cast your gaze my way like a tightly woven net.
I Astraeus, was your husband, god of the dusk,
father of the four winds,
your children in another lifetime.

Epically united, we would never part ways again.
So it seemed.

Each day I would contentedly sleep in your bosom.
At night I would rise and pat my children's heads
before I left for work, moving the stars and the
waters of the Earth around.
After you woke up the world you stayed home
and made a pretty face while the kids played outside,
creating hurricanes, water spouts, shipwrecks, and
all sorts of destructive nonsense.

So, how long did you think
I was going to put up with that?
We both know star-crossed lovers never last.
Rarely do such fanciful stories
end happily ever after.

The humble act of taking time for one's self is the ultimate kindness to the world. Seeking to be right sized I occupy my proper place in the universe.

Part Two

Slothful
Miscreants

Slothful Miscreants

Early Spring sunshine bathes Cleopatra's white shoulders
laid bare in the cool morning air.
No time left to lull in lethargic slumber,
she greets the dawn with disdain.

Thrown back covers and abruptly opened curtains
shock the queen's senses to attention.
Nibbles on her earlobes and a few soft kisses
are the best alarm clocks.

Birds chirping and noisy dogs barking combined with
distant market sounds intrude upon blissful,
dull-eyed splendor in the sheets.
"Please Anthony, might we be reprieved from rising just a little
while longer?" she whines.

My cold hands find purchase on her helpless frame.
Our eyes lock and she remembers why she loves me.
Warm and inviting as a summer night
on her barge in the Nile she seems so irresistibly delectable.
She pulls me closer once more before she tastes the day.

I protest that I must get ready,
but duty can wait, she selfishly insists.
The aroma of freshly brewed Karkade tea beckons us,
but our minds are elsewhere
as we tumble back in bed,
slothful miscreants in love.

Squander the Day

A lazy face I wore in the mirror this morning
as I washed the cobwebs from my eyes, but
this slothful mood would not give way to wakefulness.
Two cups of jet fuel and several encouraging kisses later
I began day dreaming again, as easily
as if I had never awakened.

See the tiny restless birds flit around the back yard.
The morning is still.
My hilltop temple refuge is silent as I sit in useless lethargy.
The only waking up sounds are that of
bacon crackling in an iron skillet and
the reliably steady hum of a ceiling fan,
which momentarily combine to lull me back into a dream state.
Another cup of coffee might do the trick,
perhaps a less comfortable spot from which to greet sunrise.

Standing heavy-eyed and listing sharply,
the chair on the back porch
reaches up to drag me down into its plush cushions.
Forgotten are my bills, duties and commitments.
Gone are all the chores begging for my participation.
Responsibilities are on holiday, general claims on my attention
briefly suspended, timetables lapsed, schedules run amok.
My mental list of things to do has angrily tromped off
leaving me alone with the consequences of doing nothing.

Take the Lighter Path

Tanned brown bodies follow noses
where a summer breeze directs them,
thin legs tread primordial trails,
gone exploring for their pleasure.
Two paths fork dividing sharply
all the shade from sunny spaces.
Eager eyes desire the lighter path
around the bend to see what's there.

The lighter path plies tunnel walls
of moss bound trees and thorny brush
along a green and timeless bayou
where wind-stirred grasses smoothly ripple,
heedless of both time and tourists.
On a warm summer's evening
fearless feet will always dare to tread.

Hear the crickets buzz in unison
with the droning of cicadas,
matched machine-like syncopations
both distract them and delight.
Familiar rattle and dull hum
like spoons caught in the disposal.
Delightful racket for a two scout outing.

Smell the warm air waft in fragrant bites
roasting river mud, tasty gumbo cooking.
The moist winds fan and mix the air
till it whets their appetites.
No clod or furrow will be spared
a parching from the sunshine
broken ground etched deep like cobwebs
in the baking, blackened mud.

Take it all in, pleasant freshness
on a path so rich and loamy,
freely daring all upon this earth
to take the time to tread.
Jewel backed spiders play with silver strings,
bar the shadowed path before them.
Caught off guard, resolve undaunted, they proceed to forge ahead.

Heady perfume seeps from somewhere,
pale white saprophytes uncovered.
Ghostly shaded fairy flower pipes,
half mushroom and half jasmine.
They erupt from rotting tree trunks
buried in the moldering litter,
out of place like a full moon afloat in sunny daytime skies.

Greedy summer sun plants kisses
on bare shoulders with red lipstick.
Rich brown bodies long to take their leave
from a warm and radiant Sol.
Tan feet tread the moist trail searching
for the next signs of adventures
down new paths yet undiscovered walking barefoot and divine.

Sitting at Her Mirror (2)

Sitting at her mirror this morning she frowned.
Another silver strand had found its way
to the crest of her auburn locks.
Will you still love me when I am old and gray,
she coyly asked.
Not one silver hair, or two or a thousand
could ever stop me from loving you, he replied.
She smiled appreciatively at him in her mirror.
Then she gave him her special wink of approval.
He knew that once more his words had pleased her.

Tiny wrinkles graced the corners of her lovely upturned eyes.
Not as young as I used to be,
she half whispered, apologetically.
Worry spread, her beautiful face darkened.
It seems these years have quickly passed, he said.
The little changes have escaped me, mostly unnoticed,
but to me you are more lovely than ever.
How lucky a man I am to have her,
he thought, as once more her reflection
beamed back lovingly at him.

Snapshot of Humanity

Day is an empty vessel to be constantly filled with meaningless duties.
Nameless faces attempt to frown, then smile, pensively laugh.
They nod their wooden heads. Sawdust runs out of their ears.

Maddening logic that is illogic spews forth from a wide mouth.
Flaming lips tattooed on a posing blank mannequin's face.
She holds up a mirror and sufficiently satisfied flashes white alligator teeth.

The Boss barks terse orders: employees writhe in their squeaky office chairs.
The ordeal they endure is like having needles placed in their eyeballs.
Loud exhales and naughty salutes burst forth when her door finally slams shut.

Someone vomited in the bathroom again. Third time it happened this week.
Tried not to gag, stepped around the puddle to the sink, quickly washed my hands and fled.
Pressure cooker tension boils the atmosphere, leaves an acrid smell of frazzled, frying nerves.

Tiny nobodies beg to leave work early again.
Crass ultimatums spear them in their tracks.
Meek little persons retreat to their cells and cry.
Resentful witnesses skittishly cower.
Fainthearted friends offer no condolence.

Outside streets bustle.
Mad, furious traffic rushes by a serpentine sidewalk.
A crowd congeals around a stiffly laid out drunk.

Is he dead, they wonder loudly among themselves.
Having seen no blood Great Humanity resumes filing past.

Decrepit stairways creak beneath aching feet.
Sore knees complain loudly.
Blessed end to the grueling day is just a few steps away.
The key turns. The knob twists.
Indignation turns to apathy as the door quietly closes
for the night.

Listen to the Waters
of the Bayou Sing

Take the well-worn path past the Muscadine vines.
Walk along a leveed bank where the bayou flows.
There a cypress tree standing all alone
on a rise in the middle of the tow bar grows.

Stand beneath the shade where the blackbirds roost
in the ancient live oak trees planted in a ring.
Hear the bullfrogs croak and the marsh bird's call.
Let your heart hear the songs the muddy waters sing.

Rosy spoonbills wade, alligators swim
where the blue and yellow irises so thickly thrive.
Watch a raft of ducks drifting slowly by:
makes a country boy feel happy just to be alive.

When the hot noon sun blazes overhead
time to try another tumbler of some ice cold tea
in your rocking chair, with a piece of pie.
Let that southern way of living be your recipe.

Grandma's house was old but so well preserved
it was passed down through her family generations back.
All the souls that grew up and died there knew
they were poorer, yet in nothing did they ever lack.

Chickens, pigs and beef they most proudly raised,
kept a garden, grew tomatoes, tilled the marshy land.
Prowled the broad bayous for their fish and game,
made their living from most anything they found at hand.

Grandad sent his sons to a school back east.
Hoped they'd find a better future than his family had.

On the paths they chose, up the ranks they rose,
but they hardly came to visit and that made him sad.

Modern lives they lived were a world away.
Nothing back there in the bayou could have drawn them home.
They had bright careers, came by once a year,
let the old folks work the farm land they would someday own.

All the neighbors came when their Grandad died.
They brought dishes they prepared and on that day it rained.
When the boys arrived and the wake was held
neighbors came by to console them and they shared their pain.

Now the farm is gone, Grandma long since passed.
Briars took over the pastures and the fence is down.
Someone bought the land where the homestead stood,
hailed from Birmingham, or Houston or some larger town.

The brown bayou flows and the marsh birds wade.
The wild irises still bloom along its banks each spring.
Can you see them sway in the balmy breeze,
Can you hear the muddy waters of the bayou sing?

Symphony in Crickets, Major

Don't you love to hear the crickets
in the hollows and the thickets
telling rhymes to all the creatures
underneath the evening skies.
Their insistent syncopations
make for marvelous relations
between pale white meadow flowers
and floating butterflies.

All those ne'er-do-well cicadas
in each summer will invade us.
They throw roaring office parties,
then are silent for nine years.
Strange soft husks they make and leave,
weird shapes that we shall retrieve,
dead monsters we pretend alive,
to dangle on our sleeves.

Mayflies find their daily cover,
in the millions clouds they hover.
From the marshes and the swampy spots
they fly to find their mates.
For two weeks about they flutter,
on our windscreens they will clutter.
Sticky green splotches left behind
that we are loath to clean.

In the darkness fireflies gather
for the evening's great palaver.
Bullfrogs chorus in the hundreds;
alto screech owls try soprano.
Far off alligators growling
hear the coyotes baleful howling.
Symphonies proudly played with bold
cacophonies of noise.

Therapy

A North wind stirs the waters
on the shore of a dark green bay.
Inbound waves wear whitecaps
on a late November day.

On this stretch of beach deserted,
left alone with the wind that sighs.
Long rollers march in staggered ranks
till they blend with the evening skies.

The chill of Autumn air proclaims
not long will Winter wait.
The seabirds fly to find a roost
before it grows too late.

These barren dunes speak solitude,
a haven where I go.
Both time and troubles melt away
as the tide laps to and fro.

To sand and surf none can compare,
a natural therapy,
For a troubled mind or lonely heart
they never fail to free.

Sleepwalking Through Your Dream

My dreaming feet want to walk where
you lie sleeping.
But, you would not notice me
in your innocent slumber.
Inside your lovely head fantastic, animate
dreams reel forth,
enrapturing, captivating,
running and shouting,
leaping and laughing.
My interruption would be impossible
to forgive.
I cannot bear to disturb you with my query.
If I was a dream, your dream come true,
would you wish me there beside you,
blithely sampling my kisses,
greedily inhaling all my essence
till you knew the inescapable truth:
that I was just your possession.
That I could not exist
only alive in your fantasies of us.
Sleeping there, you may never know
what might have been an epic love.
Forgive me if I go on
living without ever knowing.

Comes the Answer

Comes the question to all one day,
posed in a general sort of way.
How shall I live,
by sword or by pen,
stable without, seething within,
slave to the duties of life,
family, children, a loving wife,
or free as the beckoning wind?

Comes the answer one fine day,
clear, concise, with powerful sway.
Follow your dreams,
your ciphers and schemes
just get in the way.
Stay in the now,
it all works out somehow.
Forget it and let it be.

Waste a Day

Waste a day.
Tear up the bills.
If your house burns down while you are away
dance a jig in the ashes.

Speak your mind.
Make a scene.
If the boss gets cranky go home early.
Any day can be Friday.

Act the fool.
Run naked through the streets.
If they catch you without clothes on
tell them you were born that way.

Sleep in.
Yawn and stretch.
Throw out the alarm clock, turn off your cell.
You've no time to waste conforming.

Desire made us.

Love nurtures us.

Fulfillment spurs us on.

But, romance completes us.

Part Three

Love Builds
Its Own
Universe

Loved Beyond Measure

The voyeur in us feels no shame watching you.
We keep all secrets equally well,
whomever is the owner of them.
As you display your subtler faults to us,
no regrets should you harbor.
Do not pull down the shades on your inglorious accomplishments,
bearing harsh resentments and condemning those inadequate
existences.
Those haunted spirits of the past shared your tenement life through
other, sorrier days passed; be unashamed.
We are all born at least once to events beyond us.
Should you allow us to see your worst failures,
we promise not to lock their memory away
in a closed, pitiless heart.

Boldly display your agonizing moments of doubt
timidly lived, having survived only by way of cowardice and guile.
For what seemed ages you held up your fears like a battle shield,
broke the siege of your uncertainty with a
most distinguished lack of elegance.
Those moments, won or lost, fascinate us.

You have become the least common denominator
of humanity, a human singularity,
decisively unique, un-duplicated.
Peacocks seem drab perched beside your bright feathers.
Your guileless simplicity lends grace to a listless world
fixated on flash, image and decorum.

The renowned restauranteur often fails to recognize that
his novice chef in the making is washing the pots and pans.
Often, the arrival of one who is so genuine and substantial
is ignored, only later to be loudly proclaimed.

The humblest of lives may transcend all others.

Let us feel your trembling heart shake down
the mountains again.
May its pounding split open the sleepy earth,
wake the dead trapped in their their boring, hopeless dimensions.
Vibrate the air with your warm breath's steady syncopation.
Allow us to trace your footfalls, to endure your cuts and bruises,
absorb the pain as your feet tear open, as together we
walk bare footed over your broken dreams.

Let us watch you as if for the first time,
embrace the skies so sweetly
that tears fall from happy angels' eyes.
Make us know that we are loved beyond measure.

Mother Sky

Gathering lights of dawn take pause at their inception.
Gentle drops of rain begin to scatter shadows.
An unborn dreary daybreak in the making yawns.
Sprinkling billows lithely drift in muted moonlight,
teardrops softly falling from sleepy Cherubs' eyes.
They weep joyfully for on this day of gladness
their time has come to hasten flowers into bloom.

Prismed light paints over landscapes softly glowing.
Green and glistening, lush or fallow incandescence.
Lasers melt the sharp honed edges of the darkness.
Seamless midnight world is cast away abandoned.
Earth transforms its shape and slithers on its stomach.
Liquid legs of flowing ripples slowly wiggle
as Aurora stoops to lavish light upon her world below.

Radiant glimmers coat the branches and the sagebrush,
purge away the drab night's shadows of their secrets.
Vague forms hunkered down and hiding are discovered
camping under twinkling stars, escape confounded.
Wanton fugitives await their long due pardons.
Sol their barrister resumes the fight to free them.
They will safely steal away again when precious night returns.

Streets and sidewalks slide and ripple in the half-light.
Day breaks plastered to an opaque hostile ceiling.
Pastels peek through gloomy windows that need washing.
Weakly glowing rays elbow their ways through storm clouds.
Packed in thickly, roughly shoving and resisting,
their night's labors left unfinished, thronged together,
each perturbed and holding grudges with each other.

In a melancholy mood the heavens break ranks.
Angry house maids toss mop water onto roof tops.
Mighty rivers flow on currents caught by moonbeams.
Noisy thunder sings laments to sleeping hayfields
of the slumbering night now passed away and dreaming.
Fat and pregnant rainclouds brood together grumbling.
They display distended bellies nearly bursting to the ground.

Countless fetal lakes they clutch in angry outbursts.
Myriad unborn streams and rivers, creeks and branches,
an ocean swelled by waves of air which writhe within them.
Noisy grousing clouds sit pouting in discomfort,
poised and ready for their birth waters to rupture,
gushing forth on thirsty plains and panting prairies.
They bring precious life to all their earthbound children,
newborn puddles left to bathe in muddy bassinets.

The Longing

The bedroom's walls expand and contract in creaking darkness.
Heavy sighs punctuate
interminable silent moments alone in my bed.
Endless black shifting shadows run amuck.
Their giggles offend my senses in the clinging darkness.
Dragged down go the days gloomy specters of doom
into Night's hollow, greedy depths.

Ravenous nocturnal shades devour
the slightest flicker of candles lit against them.
No hope left for the timid glowing,
their protests silenced, quickly snuffed out.

Evening's meager dimness has timidly retreated
to hide and gnash its teeth,
whining and muttering nonsensical mantras,
fearing it may never find the courage to glow again.

Shunned is the cool elegance of fine satin sheets,
or low-backed evening gowns that cling.
Their pleated decadence calls to mind coffin liners.
Vague swaths of cool nothingness wound about my
clammy body grip me, suffocating me, helplessly
sewn up in the sheets of a burial shroud.

The persnickety bed creaks and complains.
My restless movements disturb its precarious balance.
One side politely poised, utterly empty,
the other yearning to be filled.
A yawning gulf of wanting, and not having
in between.
No love could abide in this place,
as cold and heartless as an undertaker's slab.

I beg Night be gone and relief
to return to my passionless bones.
A forsaken dawn sneers in disdain.
Rays of hope fade in the darkness of despair
as this incipient loneliness consumes me.

A soul stained Prometheus, my ruined visions haunt my
conscience.
I clamp my icy grip onto the bedpost and writhe.
My vain and fitful attempts at slumber
are denied by this preternatural ache,
this despondent longing to break free of these chains.
The Furies have deeply sunk their talons in me.
Their vulture wings violently resist my escape.
They remain despondently affixed
as they eagerly pick at my liver, that grows back every day.
No lover alive could send them scurrying back
to their dark roosts on Olympus.

See the unrumpled pillow, a matched twin,
set uselessly beside the other,
both accomplices to this wretched pain,
this brooding, wrenching want.
Need rains in buckets, freely flowing
like tears at a baby's funeral.

Won't dawn come and take away
this infernal desperation.
My bed has become an inky vortex of blackness,
a meeting place for lovers and fools
whose hope it was to be delightfully ensnared,
but found far less than they could
or should have ever imagined.

First Date

We stood
so close I thought
you were my shadow.
We touched,
your hand was trembling
oh so gently.
The sparks
were playing back and forth
between us.
Your skin
smelled rich like wine
I drank in deeply.
Your lips,
so warm and soft
they made me quiver.
We kissed,
the moments passed us
by unnoticed.
We held
each other close.
No words were needed.
You sighed,
and then I knew that
you were mine.

The Two of Them

Saint Kristi wears her smile with ease.
Wise and witty, she owns a golden crown.
Her stilled stone relief prays faithfully,
loosely holding rusty keys to his hidden heart.
She kneels nearby and waits for him always
as sweet love songs play elsewhere,
while other couples dance and laugh
she mends his shirts and dreams.

The evening star gleams in her eyes, never dull,
always glad when she spies him standing close, like her shadow.
They embrace as they dance in each other's arms,
pirouetting, dipping and forgotten is the cold, hard day.
Chaos and drama recede into
their dusty day-dreamed dimension.
All angst allayed, nothing else matters,
but the two of them, happy again.

Each of them is one, each possessed of intrigues and wants.
Root and stem they live entwined, growing, changing, thriving.
Their relationship has legs, lock-stepping as they wander.
Their wise roots grow together by design.
A compass with a crooked hand directs them imperfectly.
They are never lost.
They both know the way to one another's heart.

Forgive to Forget

Lonely tourists, we met on the road to nowhere.
You said you knew my face,
but could not remember my name.
When the revelation arrived,
you looked away in shame.
Disgraced, you hurriedly walked away.

We had no quarrel, yet you felt compelled to flee.
There was no dark sin to hide,
no just cause for your evasiveness.
What we shared was over before it had begun.
Imagined regrets intervened
before any reason ever existed.

My self-flagellation took too long.
I swallowed treble hooks,
then tried to cough them up.
I forgave you your part in it long ago,
but not with ease.
Guilty thoughts pummeled my emotions,
self-depreciation abraded my shiny veneer.
In my desperation I released you and my life got better.

Aspiring Moon

Aspiring moon shines stark and brightly tinged
with silver.
The broken shards of scattered moonlight slice
the snow caps.
No breeze builds, the sun weans day of all
its brightness.
Bent back clouds cast purple shadows on
the mountains.
Warm wind whispers silent rumors of
new seasons.

Birds make haste for havens sheltered in
the valleys.
Looming conifers mount slopes that
stand majestic.
Stone faced, buttressed tors hide aeries in
their bosoms.
Mule deer forage beneath seeding stands
of Pinons.
They are drawn by high lights placed in skies
to guide them.

Salmon swim in deep carved glacial lakes
in winter.
They seek mayfly swarms of millions for
the feasting.
They arrive two weeks in May to reap
the bounty.
How they know the time the greatest
mystery.
God and salmon know great fishermen
never tell.

At great abundance they rejoice with
new found zeal.

Fauna paid uncounted tolls in slow
starvation.
Slopes erupt in bloom a short time in
the mountains.
Blossoms speckled powdered hillsides with
black berries.
Air is filled with subtle sweetness, scent
of fortunes.
All will share the juicy harvest at
their leisure.

Tender twigs will sate till switch grass is abundant
on the slopes.
They seek shade from suns hung carelessly above the
azure skies.
In this haven free of hunters, both the four legged
and the two.
By primordial plan they raise their chicks, and calves
and hatchlings.
Aspiring Moon has brought them joys that reach beyond their
wildest dreams.

The King Sun Approaches

Soughing winds precede the dawn in the wee hours.
Stars retreat to light their homes in soot black heavens.
Pregnant moon mounts Summer Solstice skies in twilight.
Fireflies flee to hide with inky gloom departing.
Toads and crickets loud lament the shortened night time.
They seek cover from approaching hours of swelter
as Earth's star sheds warmth on harshly wilted meadows.
Grounds they crawl upon will soon endure a parching.
Terra firma has split open in a heat wave.
In a million crisscrossed cracks the land is fractured.
Shriveled grasses beg for any small libation.
Morning dew will soothe their slowly scorching palates.

Shadows wither in the glare of searching headlights.
Black, grey, silver phantoms stalk the blighted hedgerows.
Heavy shadowed and dull hued stand stately houses.
Down the street they loom like large and hulking masses.
Their windows turn askew revealing landscapes sparsely laid.
For brief moments they leap out to grab the spotlight,
stark profiles caught up in bright illumination.
Just as quickly they turn back to charcoal substance.
Omnipresent, they persist in darkling portrait.
Concealed worlds will guard their presence cloaked in shadows.
Coolly clutched black muslin curtains made of darkness
hide all substance since returned to rule the morning.

Even dim light changes all it softly brushes.
Rosy sunbeams roust the peaceful rest of specters.
Silhouetted ghostly figures rustle bushes.
Silver, grey, then black leaves flutter fanned by Zephyrs.
Dancing, quaking limbs are shaken to attention.
Birds stir from their roosts in greeting for their ruler.
They sing loudly, He is here now! He is here now!

King Sun rises inexorably above his subjects.
He comes home to brightly cheer them every morning.
Lording with a steady grace he gives their hearts hope
as he mounts the sky this glorious day he's made.
Happy in his rein his smile beams joy and pleasure
upon all his Earth bound subjects there below.
He returns once more to rule their waking hours,
come with dignity and power for the masses.
Grace enough for all he grants with warmth and kindness.
He rules mighty as his world turns on its axis,
smiling up in adoration of their hero,
their new King has brought the light to all his subjects.
He smiles down once more and winks at passing clouds.

Other Worlds, Other Languages

All the world proclaims itself in different voices
soft or harsh, or untranslatable to many.
We may guess, but few can hear what they are saying.
Every sound and noise reveals another message.

Utter silence, paused or lasting, makes its statement,
though the quiet whispered phrases sound like static.
Overarching looms the roar of raging rivers
while the stones, the trees and mountains play their music.

Tides rush in like minstrel singers crooning love songs.
Sweet perfection we take in, then take for granted.
Wild wind's howls or sallow soughs concert unheeded.
Black-branched, telegraphed loud clicks and clacks dispatch.

Brown leaves rustle like maracas in the treetops.
Verdant forests echo every living heartbeat.
Barely noticed sings the chorus in the forest
while we madly dash through muddled, mundane musings.

Our ears strain to hear some message from above us.
Still unsure, we beg for answers we can cling to.
Clues arrive, but in an unfamiliar language,
spoken to our hearts with hope that we might hear.

More Than You Can Stand

When you need to be a saint
and you are only a man.

Her face, her eyes
are killing you.

You respect her feelings
but she does not understand.

Her lips, her kiss
are thrilling you.

You need her and
it is more than you can stand.

Love of My Life

Hello my lover, my comforter, my soft embrace.
The giver of warm hugs and hot kisses
wrapped in a love song, sung a cappella.
Your words strum the strings to my heart till the cold blood melts.
Those silent words have conquered my heart.
Croon sweetly your ancient, mysterious ballads
that lovers practice lifetime after lifetime,
hoping to memorize your sacred chants.

Once more Athena's feathered avatar sings to me
through her rapturous eyes,
patiently teaching me her wordless tunes
of longing for and having,
of lacking and finding.
The full moon in her eyes serenades me.
Great hungers within claw at my stomach, biding time,
waiting to be shared again.

In other lives of endless nights we danced in the bacchanal.
You meticulously prepared the festivities.
Toneless, flavorful words became our scrumptious repast.
You were my caterer, chef, waitress, dinner partner.
We shared a silent entrée, lavishly prepared, richly seasoned.
Now you tread new grapes as the carnival is readied.

Your statue dances and twirls again
in my dreaming mind's eye.
You are more real than I could ever be.
Touch me again, healer of my flagging faith.
Spawn laughter in my humorless bones.
Confer your highest honors, Dean of Delights,
Doctor of Deliciousness,
unbound and generous upon the likes of me.

Build me up, architect of my happiness.
Cornerstone of my world, bless this humble house.
Construct me with a firm foundation
able to weather tempest or quaking.
Like mortar in the cracks
of my character, bind yourself to me.

May the gods in their mercy allow me to live
another long life with you,
to relearn the wonder and complexity, the all of you.
You are the love of my life,
my darling wife.

Icing on the Cake

She gazed into her
dressing room mirror.
A bit of white streaked
her long full locks.
Are you still attracted to me,
she asked, eyes coyly down cast,
somewhat forlorn.

I paused and remembered all
those bygone years.
That's just icing on the cake,
I answered with a wink
as I pulled her into my arms
for one more delicious taste.

Had He Not Failed at Love (1)

Had he not failed at love,
he would not have known
about the great void,
the deep, dark pit,
the yawning cavity
at the center of a nothing person,
living a nothing life, going nowhere.

Swallowing his fears and regrets
he dwelled bereft of peace, hardly dreaming.
He would not have known about his emptiness.
Inside was a chasm, too wide to span, too huge to fill.
In vain he groped for any panacea to heal his wasted life.
He accumulated a mountain of empty promises
he had made to a tyrant God.
Then he became the Tyrant.
He denied himself all forms of friendship.
As the void fed on him, he grew emptier.

The miser in him set aside all of the simple pleasures
that others take for granted.
Petty things like having hot water for bathing,
a pet as a companion against the loneliness,
the heartless master rejected as undeserved richness.
Clouds obscured his sun and moon: directionless wandering persisted.
The monster in him growled at any and all who approached.
He felt great ambivalence toward his old friends whose lives had passed
him by on their way to somewhere called success.
At their approach he growled, be gone! You are not welcome here!

A chronically broken man stood aghast at his reflection,
a fractured creature railing from the bowels of a fetid swamp,
sinking ever deeper into the mire of his wasted life.

Unworthy. His peers had become a flock of magpies cawing
out his shame and failures to a disinterested world.
Their warm words and encouragements pecked away at him
mercilessly, leaving him a deeper distrust of everything he was told.
In a life totally consumed by self
no significant other could ever have existed.

His shadow crept away from those closest to him.
His absence was unmissed.
Fantastic beliefs consumed his thoughts.
Lost in his misguided beliefs, the rest of him went missing.
His wants were unsent letters, useless papers.
Parents, lovers, friends,
all absent or undiscovered, hazy shadowbox images
of lives best left abandoned and forgotten.
So the great void within him swallowed up his past,
greedily nibbled at his future.

Just a boy of twelve,
he had lost his loving grandmother,
struck down one fateful morning
by a drunk driver in her cups.
For childish reasons he had chosen
not to walk with her to the market that day.
The stark finality of death numbed him to living.
Her tragic demise grew him, warped him into adulthood.

Had he been there, and he blamed himself
for not being there,
God might have allowed him
to die with dignity, as well.
Guilt is the grownup legacy
of a childhood poorly lived.
His useless pleas to the Fates went unanswered.
Of what worth was one old woman's life to an apathetic world

bereft of sentiment and grace? He was guilty.
An uncaring world had judged him unworthy of love.

He vowed that for his lifetime he would never love again.
Undying guilt became the casualty of shame.
He was hostage to both.
It would slowly ease as enough blood flowed.
As self-loathing cruelly replaced his shame,
he felt the vultures firmly set their claws into his psyche.

Decades crept by at glacial speed
while his youth perished and manhood emerged
from the dark cave of uncertainty.
Desperately groping for salvation,
he found the crusty cork
and plunged it back into the bottle.
The Jinn was once again imprisoned.
The new sun was terrible to behold.
His flesh felt seared by its loving touch,
a touch he somehow recognized as vital.
His flyspecked mirror cleared momentarily
as a foggy image focused.
Through the haze he watched his past life wave goodbye.
Old beginnings were ended, new endings had begun,
and in that moment he realized that
no one ever firmly recognizes which is which.

Had He Not Failed at Love (2)

He felt no sorrow
for vagabond lovers forlorn and meek, or
lovers lost in the fog of life's pageant of mysteries.
He tried to swaddle the gentle spirited and
sick of heart who languished,
slowly disappearing
from excessive loneliness.
In the end, he felt no pity for them.

Neither did he pine for the
overly obsessed and fearful little girls he had set his heart on,
nor their desperate parents who pulled them away,
unwilling to take a chance
on someone like him,
another unwanted gift casually left on their doorsteps.
He could not blame them.
He knew what he was. Pariah.

Times were hard and couples married young,
had children, then promptly
forgot they were in love.
Their friends were soon derelicts, as well.
They drove down blind alleys till
their failures and obsessions flattened their tires.
The divorces that followed did not help them
love each other more.

He could find no pity for the sacrificed families he knew.
Valkyries took their heroic sons and daughters
off to Valhalla.
Many died in unjust wars on foreign soil.
To protect their children they wrapped them in the flag,
but they died anyway, not knowing for whom,

or for what purpose, they had martyred themselves.
They did not ask for his condolences, or his judgment.
They had his respect.

He would regret forming all
those hasty, awkward friendships.
He fast grew fond of many: just as quickly
they were displaced by his perpetual grief.
Sometimes they plunged together through
life's creeks and rivers.
Like a bad egg he always bobbed to the top
and kept swimming.
Some never resurfaced,
while with others, for him it was just as well
that they did not.

Car wrecks sometimes claimed their dignity,
leaving them so damaged
that their trauma was always in the forefront.
He witnessed jagged scars on the cheek
of a cherub-faced girl he adored.
Her inner battles had bloodied her.
She showed no one the deeper cuts on her heroic heart.
Athena in rags, she stood tall and proud
as her temple burned to the ground around her.
In worship he fell to his knees, openly weeping.

Though she never returned his fervent love,
she never turned her back on him.
She always made a place for him at her table.
An open door greeting him when he visited.
She gently placed kind words in his granite ears,
sharing her love with him till he could find his own.
He sat happily pondering his life in front of her shrine.
Wise Athena beamed at him as grateful tears fell
upon dusty white marble steps which needed sweeping.

I Need to Hear Something

Let me hear audacious mumblings from you.
Your hungry glances are not enough to sate me.
Wistful words invite and entice when whispered in the dark.
Like cotton candy they are scrumptious,
not enough to satisfy--say I love you, too.

Sometimes, in another dream, I run away from you.
The special someone who really cares for me becomes a Harpy.
Questions and complaints incessantly pass your lips.
You dishevel my bookshelf life,
thrown down volumes scattered about,
everything in hopeless disarray.

It took a lifetime to put it all in place,
then I found you.
Perseus spied Andromeda.
I was ready to battle the Kraken.
Feels like I crawled through hell to win you.
I would gladly go there again to be with you.
Ask Chiron to hold the ferry for me.

So, should I ever go mad and abandon
the very best life I ever lived, please
call me back, pick me up, dust me off.
Help me limp home to you, my Venus.

Don't forget your soft lap for my pillow.
Bring along your arms next time to hold me tightly.
I never tire of hearing your charming white lies.
Fill your pocket full of kind words to strew about.
Bring those gentle kisses you always have handy just for me.

She Mourns My Inattention

I heard her moan as teardrops began falling.
Silently she tried to mourn my inattention, but failed.
What has become of my poor, dear husband?
She uttered a sigh in deep despair.
The song in my heart is forever silenced.
He will never come again to light my empty life.
Once again she yearns for my strong embrace, a tender touch.
Spirit can only reach so far from this time and place.

Albums full of photographs and fond memories
never pictured a day when the present moment would seem so
far from yesterday.
Now is when we need, when we yearn, hold our breath for love.
It is now that speaks loudest into the darkness
of our memories.
Then is quieter and weaker, biding its time to chime in.
Then reminds us of better times, chides us that those times
are no more, will never be again.
Pessimistically inclined, then causes the heart to ache
from missing, longing, yearning for what we had,
while now goes away to hover just out of reach.

Dear wife, if we could have had any day over again,
what we had back then,
could we have done better with it?
This was always meant to be,
to deny it just a vain wish, selfishness,
a rude, off-putting occurrence,
unplanned for and unwanted.
"What if" is another exaggerated set of lies we tell ourselves,
as though we might have always remained joined in some other
intimately physical sense.

Hold your hand a little closer to the picture.
Tenderly caress the frame: take your time.
I am there somewhere near, and far away, in the same moment.
Eternally shared, a love like ours can never fade completely.
I never pondered leaving you in such a state of nothingness, yet,
here we are.

My image still smiles back at you from behind the glass covered
window that provides you a glimpse at my past being,
forever changed.
Feel me blow a kiss toward your glistening cheek.
Warm and willing you have always been.
Soft and tender is each kiss I send.
Cry if you must, but I still smile when I think of loving you.
There is no sorrow great enough to take away the love we knew.
No set of circumstances could replace the life we lived together.
Never again is too broad a statement for a love like ours.
Never is such a long way from now.

Concentrate.
Fix it in your mind, what cannot be,
yet seems so real.

Hear.
Let the peaceful sounds fill you. Empty your
ringing head full of noises.

Savor.
There is much more to appreciate in all we
see and hear than can ever be dreamed or
imagined.

Part Four

Homespun
World Views
and
Altered Histories

Winter Painting

Winter paints with ice and snow
upon the fields and water ways
scenes of beauty, gloss and glimmer.
Chill winds make a palette
for the frost to play.

White swirled powder on dun yellow stubble.
Blue ice border frames the lake shore's rim.
Beneath the leaden hoarfrost
that trims sleeping branches,
cast silver gilded statues of stems and limbs.

Earth's grey domed ceiling erupts in golden splendor.
Magenta clouds spill purple shades
where light and darkness meet.
Oranges, reds and pink pastels adorn the lofty heavens.
Scarlet billows blossom as the light of day retreats.

Stark yellow moonrise on an iridescent landscape,
Charcoal etched tree trunks tinged in dull shaded grey.
Golden tongues lick chocolate logs
roasting in the fireplace,
reflecting pleasant silhouettes of a perfect Winter day.

Victorious Night

The nocturnal world has no equal in its power,
shares no title with the day, bright or dimming.
Sundown ruthlessly deposes all it ponders
as a darkened world sits by loudly applauding.
The dark Night, the grand usurper
boldly struts forth to acclaim.

Shadow and pitch black contrive a pact,
united in earnest consternation.
With fading sunlight's final rays
Night's onslaught is complete,
save for vague chips, flashing diamonds
glued onto a charcoal canvas hung above.

Aimless casual wisps of cosmos drift by slowly,
ineffectual glitter and tinsel, at their best.
The dingy lens of a sleepy world is out of focus.
Molten glass, poorly cast, thickly covered in grey ash.
A distorted, star smudged window framed in blackness,
with its shades draw tightly down.

As the tangible acquiesces to invisible,
unknowns hold advantage for a while.
From any grassy hilltop floating flecks of fire drift by
on silent wings, buoyed up by a wafting, wistful breeze.
Brief flashes of beacon signals harmlessly buzz
the phantom sleeping meadows.

A restless, shining city beckons below the towering rim rocks.
Red and yellow snakes slowly creep, slithering
through the canyons' high cut walls.
Light and darkness bravely tussle for dominion.
Miles of marching midnight shadows
piqued by headlights join in battle.

The road that was bends and curves toward the blackness.
In retreat vanquished beams cross vague horizons.
Another pitiful flash of a star falls barely noticed,
streaking across the sparkling heavens, fading to nothing.
Meager offerings of the glowing are rejected
by penumbral depths of Night now in command.

Fires in Mexico

Once reliable rays of dawn are squelched by rafts of haze
as verdant forests in Mexico uncontrollably burn,
nesting grounds of Monarch butterflies
that flock there in the millions.
The timid sun chokes on soot and ash.
Events and their aftermaths are separated by a thousand miles.
Like ghosts from a long buried past the toxic pallor arrives,
smoky wisps of havoc still smoldering somewhere down South.
Vague, shapeless consequences now come to visit.
Into my dull napping life they intrude.
Like unexpected house guests
they demand all my reluctant attention.
They change all my plans without my permission.

At first I try to ignore this unwanted diversion.
Mountains always seem to sprout
where molehills once took root.
I remember that there are no more big deals for me today.
Tragedy and inconsequence are but faces on a magic coin
I carry around in my pocket and fidget with now and then.
At each decision which must be made
I toss it in the air.

Smoke and ash hang hopelessly below a resilient sun,
unperturbed and valiantly shining.
Winds of fortune may change direction overnight.
The stars remain in their places, though invisible, and splendid
above the fray.
My coin tumbles helplessly in the air as gravity does its work.
Indoors or outdoors, either way, a good day to be alive.

A Time for Everything

The end to this day was hiding and laughing behind my back.
I bent and measured time to perform all of my tasks.
Einstein would be proud of me.
I fit them all into my blinking digital time machine.
Somehow they all melded together, neatly packed into the
wormhole of my computer's hard drive.
Eat, smoke, work, rest, all carefully allocated to span
a few precious hours.
Not a moment was set aside to bleed or cry,
or see to other essential bodily functions.
A dozen interruptions could not slow the fateful hour glass.
Nothing else mattered but the schedule.

Home at last.
With outreached arms my overstuffed couch waits to coddle me
in its downy softness.
Hand me my Commander's remote.
Escape from this nightmarish press of deadlines is at hand.
Let's put out the cat and lock the door.
He needs to get out more.
We'll order a pizza, then disconnect the phone.
No cooking allowed tonight, no dishwashing, either.
Clear the bridge and draw the blinds so we can walk around naked
to God and the world if we want to.
You'll rub my Frankenstein feet,
I'll massage your Hunchback shoulders,
and anything else that hurts.
We'll hug and kiss ourselves into a remarkable oblivion.

Forgive the Night

Forgive the Night that slithers along
like an inky river of nothingness.
It fills in the plains and valleys,
with a black amalgam of matte, monotone pigment.
Devoid of essential light or any prismatic beauty,
the day is slain mercilessly, colors unhinged.
Its glow snuffed out like a hopeless candle in a gale.

Nothing remains to see or be seen.
Voided visions give way to emptiness, not peacefully.
This is Night's fundamental nature,
just as loneliness is not solemnity.
Pregnant with unforetold events,
Night cloaks the world in dreams and visions
which both disturb and titillate slumbering sojourners.

Dark, quiet terror pervades unchecked.
What was, now is not.
What is may not really be, after all.
Uncertainty and confidence are bed fellows again,
bracketed by blackest chaos.
The know all sees the know nothing,
blinks the foul image from its eyes, and flees.

Static Night

Dripping branches bow contritely to
the inky ground obscured by clammy, clinging fog.
Water falls dribble onto a dyed black lawn.
Darkness looms, having rested in the shadows.
All motion is masked by a velvety blanket of blackness.
Static night suppresses all nocturnal sounds.
Invisible stillness pervades.

Sudden activity awakens me as night creature sentries begin to stir,
breaking their quiet vigils as they
try in vain to pray the moon and stars into being.
Across the street a light comes on, a brief and pitiful glowing
interlude to the dull monotony of darkness.
The heavy ornate hands of my Mother's hall clock crawl
ponderously around the dial face as a bell chimes softly each hour
between midnight and morning as time slips sluggishly by.

Precious sleep took wing a while ago.
Flocks of worries came to roost instead.
They built noisy nests in the comfort of a peaceful rest.
Feral cats court shamelessly in the alleyway out back.
They raid the neighbor's garbage cans, raise a ruckus.
Their annoying moans and carousals are interspersed with modest
silence.

The upstairs couple is at it again wrestling on my ceiling.
Faint giggles and gasps punctuate their bedpost bump, bump,
bumping the wall.
They rhythmically declare their love for one another on a regular
basis.
Then all is gratefully still and silent once more.
Sacred sleep hides itself sniggering in the closet.

Drowse meekly delays as the stillness in the room becomes uncomfortable, suffocating.

Two doors down the nightly shouting erupts.
Someone has come home drunk again.
His shrill wife is unhappy and unleashes hell.
An hour later the cops drop by.
They officially enforce a truce and leave.
The bed is not yet ready to make peace with me.
All bets are off that slumber will ensue.
My eyelids have capitulated.
They finally droop unaided as I lapse into a peaceful, dreamless snore.

Bread in the Mouths of Modern Gods and Other Dinner Party Disasters

Pocked and shabby our finely polished surfaces have become,
badly beaten reflections of ourselves, almost unrecognizable.
A chink or two or twenty, like old teeth, have fallen out completely.
Cracked open, crumbling mouths, gagged or ignored out of
existence.
Our sibilant palates have been sealed, throats throttled, caved in.
Mighty boulders, once monuments, now turned to insignificant
pebbles having been worn down by harsh incidents and time.

No longer able to shout our discontent,
onward we roll, thump, thump, thump,
like gimpy shopping carts, making insufferable noises
anonymously limping along between supermarket aisles
barely noticed and unwanted,
destined to be ground to dust,
in history's gristmill.

With all our contradictions, and a plethora of
superfluous, obstructionist views we have become
like chaff, discarded hulls, pebbles and generally
unsavory leavings worth nothing to anybody.
The luckless majority fear to protest lest they are
swept up and pulverized, ignoble sacrifices
for the good of humanity and great press appeal.
Their bodies would become the Communion bread
of the duped masses,
their blood a spirited drink for consumption during
nightly news casts.

Popular opinion powers the grind stone
ever spinning, crushing,
till lives, events and persons become finely sifted flour,

homogenized for palatability,
chocked full of unwholesome ingredients.
Propaganda, half-truths, bold faced lies force fed
to the fiery eyed masses,
bread consuming bread, not a crumb of it wasted.

This is the bread of lies and deceit.
This is the loaf leavened with hatred and bigotry
cooked by mad chefs following "Sweeney Todd" recipes.
This is the meal that never should have happened.
Our dinner guests have slain us and bled us.
They feast on the body politic and grow thin.
This is what never would have been
had we remembered other dinner party disasters.

One notable shindig was held by the esteemed
Sir Francis Galton who invited a cousin named Charles Darwin,
along with a few less wholesome guests sporting vile appetites, to
dinner at his place.
A couple of presidents, T. Roosevelt and W. Wilson
had to bow out at the last minute
excused by the pressing business of warfare.

Dr. Josef Mengele the infamous German anthropologist, got the
invitation that was intended for Gregor Mendel the geneticist.
Having heard about the other famous invitees he really wanted to
attend, so he invited himself.
Respected Psychologist Henry H. Goddard refused to be left out
and popped in unannounced carrying copies of his latest
intelligence test for all the other guests to take home
as parting gifts.
Harry H. Laughlin, famous American stock breeder and J.H.
Kellogg, a filthy rich cereal and vitamin salesman, rode together,
arriving around the time the third sterilized course was served.
Adolph Hitler brought some strudel for dessert.
Galton's latest theory, eugenics, topped the discussion,

along with whom to blame for the ills of the world, and Hitler
made some interesting proposals they all found fascinating.
A swell time was had by all.
Others heard about Galton's dinner party and decided
to have their own.
Joseph Stalin invited 20 million of his own citizens
to a banquet in Siberia.
Accommodations were shabby, but it was still a hit.
Not to be outdone, Mao Tse-Tung invited 50 million Chinese
to his get-togethers, billed them as combination
self-improvement workshops and diet seminars.
Everyone learned a great deal from them.

To a lesser degree, many guest lists have been formulated in the
decades since, mostly by political and military leaders who
wanted to increase their popularity:
Dictators Pol Pot of Cambodia, President Augusto Pinochet of
Chile, the Shah of Iran, Mohammad Reza Pahlavi, Philippines
President Ferdinand Marcos, Syria's leader Bashar al-Assad and
Saddam Hussein of Iraq, to name a few, followed examples
of their peers.
They all showed the world how to throw swinging parties.
Their party favors were exotic as well.
IED's, barrel bombs, napalm, sarin gas missiles, chlorine cocktails
have all become effective methods in use everywhere for gaining
popularity among the citizenry.

These events are the fruit of a past that
we never expected, but feared.
The past is now starving us all,
overshadowing our futures.
The past has become the present and is compelling
us to dine on undigested facts and unsavory
assumptions that were laid down before now,
while the rest of the world gorges
on our moribund corpse.

We have become a fine repast for younger teeth,
with sharper minds and faster appetites.
Those of us the sieve missed will soon be identified as grit in the
mouths of these modern gods.
They will cruelly spit us out having determined
that we add no value to their diets.
We have become nothing more than worthless irritants after all.

Forgive

Let me speak to you about your passing, Mother.
My candle lost its glow.
The wind which blew you out was not a violent wind.
No horrible wasting away took you.
Some small token of peace can be found in that.
Do not worry about me, my Thetis.
Your Achilles will do just fine without you.
Of all the things he regrets, the worst
is not having your encouragement.

It was an empty birthday present he left on your doorstep.
Having failed to comfort you, he fled for a number of years,
too sick to seek your solace,
too proud to admit his honest shortcomings
till your ending pierced his heel like fire,
and he could run no more.
You never complained.

How helpless he felt watching your spirit flicker,
ever weaker, faintly glowing till the light in your eyes went away.
Though the shades of your dim life were drawn tightly shut
you still managed a smile as he wept,
more for himself than for you.
A responsible mother, you parented alone while his father was away.
You taught him to look out for himself and others
who had less than you had.

He soldiered in your esprit de corps till the end
an obedient, unquestioning, little brown-nosed kid.
He became his own man servant, shined his shoes
like you taught him.
You ironed his shirts and wrote
impeccable thank you letters together.

You stayed up late teaching him to spell and
worked algebra problems with him.

You taught him to tie Windsor knots, set the dinner table,
make military folds on your bed sheets.
He learned how to mop floors, practice good manners and
courtesy.
And, he took all that for granted
when he left you behind so long ago.
You taught him cash register honesty.
He became George Washington and Abe Lincoln rolled into one,
a frightened little boy trying to live in his own skin,
wrestling, like everyone else, with integrity and forgiveness.
He desperately needs those things now.

Forgive the prodigal son who beat a path to the door when he
left you behind,
before you left him behind, alone and shaken, forever.
You protected him from everything with your wisdom and
generosity.
He ran afoul of his wayward dreams and ciphers,
unable, in the end, to protect you from the sting
of your certain demise.
Forgive.

Primordial Secrets

Grey mist hangs in this chilly clime
damp and still on dismal days.
Sun comes up but will not shine,
its face obscured in the cloaking haze.

Dull light sinks to the swampy ground,
cloaked in clinging clouds of fog.
Dripping branches and soggy earth
seclude this peaty little bog.

Dank dampness chills the weary bones
of a wanderer who braves the day.
Bubbling mud makes sucking sounds;
beneath his feet the earth gives way.

Ill luck to miss the unmarked path,
no manmade sign to point the way.
No one to tell where danger lies,
so easy for the foot to stray.

Broad ripples reach across the pond,
swiftly done, none heard his cries.
The hooting owls and croaking toads,
they know just where his body lies.

The fireflies flashed his epitaph
in marshland primordial code,
another victim in the bog,
the ancient tale again retold.

The silent swamp gives up no clues,
its dead lie waiting there unclaimed.
They walk among us here no more,
their disappearances unexplained.

Freed at Last

The long fearful journey of the heart is over.
We are wed in the spirit, coupled, two halves made whole.
Let us walk away from our lonely cells released from solitude
and doubt.
All ceremony and pomp discarded, every useless, penitent ritual
is forgotten.

Excitement surges as an unknown future invites, entices.
Full of dreams forming, shapes of new hope dance in our midst.
Inklings of all our shared tomorrows seem partially revealed,
protracted and malleable.
Now we are ready to try our hands at living a new way together.

Feel the fires burn within your pulsing veins
intoxicated by this milestone's momentary bliss.
We wildly cast aside our anxious quirks and notions of love.
Discarded are the worn out rags of our former beggarly lives.

Securely paired, beautifully bonded, we stroll proudly
into the sunrise of our first shared tomorrow.
We embrace the life giving sun itself.
All nurturing, it provides new substance, erases drab
shadow lives led desperately clutching at a vague existence.

Radiance rules, blazing light lavishly emitted by hidden star fire,
light enough to melt the coldest night from our frozen hearts.
The brim of the world overflows, warm hands lift up tired limbs.
Grand raiment woven from light clothe our meek spirits in
majestic golden splendor.

The air warms as we rise upon ephemeral wings.
We bask in awe of this magnificent Spirit.

This presence entreats us, beckons us,
to a warmer path, to healing and comfort.

Freed now, we may at last learn to wholly love one another.
Equal and generous, grateful to be allied with hope as our guide
and wisdom as our benefactor, we trust our choice
was always intended from the beginning of time.

Noisy Warnings Nation

Hear a ruckus in the distance,
raucous yells and foul name calling.
Sirens sound with great insistence,
barking mutts and caterwauling.

Strike the anvil, buildings shudder,
blare of trumpets splits the cool air.
Whistles loudly spit and sputter,
geese in gaggles honking beware.

Blaring fog horns in a blue bay,
fire truck clangors down a dark lane.
Bells chime at the start of new day,
landlord taps on my front door pane.

Cell phone rings a catchy jingle,
Let's grab some lunch, where can we meet?
Horns honk while old friends intermingle,
pack the chock-blocked, crowded side street.

Neighbors wrestle, bang the thin walls,
garbage trucks crush empty trash cans.
Shouts boom down apartment's long halls:
someone cancelled dinner date plans.

Smoke alarm wails, one more burned meal;
dog next door has found his lost bone.
Car door slams shut, tires loudly squeal,
child sits sobbing, left home alone.

Church bell peels, it's time for praying;
chickens cluck, canaries peeping.

Horses neighing, donkeys braying;
really wish they all were sleeping.

Warning buzz means back to classrooms,
downcast looks display frustrations.
Caution sounds may signal the doom
of our noisy warnings nations.

Ulysses Returns Triumphant

The days are long,
the nights are restless.
My head is full of worries,
mostly things I cannot change.
It seemed like more
than I could stand today.
I subjugated Troy, but
I am still lonesome and afraid.
No one cares and
they won't let me go back home.

The triumph of adventure is not in accomplishments,
but in the accounts of our exploits told in thrilling fashion.
We hope to arrive undamaged, to recite well-rehearsed stories.
How, against long odds, we single-handedly exalted over adversity.
The more hopeless the challenge, the better the tale told.
We gleefully repeat our whimsical anecdotes, relive
our conquests, daring deeds in faraway lands
and the fascinating people we were lucky to meet.
Nobel conflicts were resolved bravely, in our favor
and exotic rendezvous secretly kept.
Not so for this brave Ulysses.

I imagine a return where no crowd will stand
cheering its conquering hero.
No ticker tape parade will stop
all the traffic on Fifth Avenue,
no carnival float to sit upon and wave to the masses.
No plush limousine will arrive
to whisk me away from the adoring throng.
Its engagement cancelled, the band will not be performing.
The bus will arrive off schedule, late as usual.
I will step to the curb alone.

I shall come to my welcome party unannounced,
doing my little victory dance.
The tunes will be boring,
the orchestra a little tone deaf,
the audience distracted, restless and apathetic.
No refunds for admission will be made available.
I shall tap my feet,
try to measure the beat,
grateful just to shuffle along the floor.

Ulysses arrives at his room renewed.
His home is inside these drab cubicle walls.
Comfortable again inside his skin
he yawns and stretches, put out the lamp.
His head rests more lightly than before
upon his pillow.
His sword and shield dutifully deposited in their proper places,
he sinks into a peaceful,
boring sleep and dreams of nothing.

A Line in the Tome of Time

I am the rhyme, the shrill wind screamed.
It crashed great waves upon the shore.
Pushed up the tide, the maelstrom swelled.
Rivers and bays could hold no more.

Rhythm am I, the earthquake boomed,
shrugged its shoulders till walls fell down.
The Mountains skipped, valleys tumbled
like rippled blankets, green and brown.

A stanza written hot and fast,
belched the volcano full of steam.
Spat out new lands, buried the past,
raised worlds beyond our wildest dreams.

Man's conscience lies there half asleep.
I'll wake him up with warning bells.
The Ocean roared, rose wide and deep,
unleashed choruses of death knells.

Through fire, and flood and blood I shape,
Nature shouted so all might heed.
Now wastes of dust and ash I make,
crack open grounds to sprout new seeds.

Mankind's a poem, short, soon passed.
Old men are not what they were young.
Sonnets and Haikus will not last,
lines in the tome of time, unsung.

Acknowledgements

Kindle Direct Publishing, kdp.amazon.com/self-publishing, from my E-book, *The Wasted Space Between Your Ears;* 2019. (Several poems taken from that E-book appear in this one as well, reworked or in their entirety and remain the property of the author).

Self-published online at allpoetry.com under author's name, Jerry Lovelady, 304 S. Jones Blvd. #191, Las Vegas, NV 89107, USA; (Some of my poetry seen here has been revised from the versions on the allpoetry.com website. All rights retained by the author).

"Fairy Tales and Fantasies"--This version was revised in 2018, first published in a poetry compilation called *Simple Truths*, Poetry Press, P.O. Box 736, Pittsburg, Texas 75686, (1998). Reprinted in E-book form, *The Wasted Space Between Your Ears*, Kindle-Amazon. (All rights retained by the author).

"Therapy"--This version republished in 2019, first published 1997, Copyright--Sparrowgrass Poetry Forum, Inc. Published by Sparrowgrass Poetry Forum, Inc., 609 Main St., P.O. Box 193, Sistersville, WV 26175: ISBN 0-923242-55-4. Poetic Voices of America; Fall Edition, 1997. (All rights retained by the author). Reprinted in E-book form, *The Wasted Space Between Your Ears*, Kindle-Amazon.

"First Date"--This version, republished in 2019; First published in Treasured Poems of America, Fall Edition, 1997 by Sparrowgrass Poetry Forum, Inc. (Library of Congress Cat. Card Numb. 90-640795. ISBN 0-923242-54-6). (All rights retained by the author). Reprinted in E-book form*, The Wasted Space Between Your Ears*, Kindle-Amazon.

"Love of My Life"--This version revised in 2018, first published 1997, as "The Love of My Life" in a poetry collection entitled *Sensations*, pg. 154, Iliad Press, an imprint of Cador Publishing, LTD. 36923 Ryan Rd., Sterling Heights, MI., 48310. ISBN--1-885206, Library of Congress Cat. No.: 97-068838. (All rights retained by the author). Reprinted in E-book form, *The Wasted Space Between Your Ears*, Kindle-Amazon.

"Forgive" –This poem was originally written for a contest created by Jan Serene called "Letters" on the poetry site, allpoetry.com. The intention was to write a letter to someone we knew telling them things we found difficult, or impossible, to say directly to them. My mother had passed away in November of 2019 and the loss was still spawning fresh grief for me.

"The Wreckage of My Zombie Past"—We are never fully clear of our pasts. If time is a continuum then all events, past and present, may perpetuate independent of one another, existing in various scenarios at one time or another, perhaps at the same time in different dimensions that may exist mere moments apart. Though we may wish for the past to go away and leave us alone, sometimes it crops up unexpectedly when we least need or wish to remember it. All events in the past are still a part of us. It is good to remember that they are what has gotten us to here and now.

"Being Here and Now"—Inspired from a book written in 1971 titled *Remember, Be Here Now*, by Baba Ram Das (Richard Alpert), a spiritual writer. It was an oddly bound paperback book full of cartoon drawings, mandala art, references to yoga, spirituality and meditation. Hippies everywhere adopted it as their bible. Kudos to my Aunt Gloria for giving me a copy. The book is still in print through HarperCollins Publishing, LLC, 195 Broadway; New York, N.Y., USA. The book has sold more than 2 million copies, according to Wikipedia.

"She Mourns My Inattention"—After my Father passed I became acutely aware of what seems to be the finality of death, and how close at hand it remains at all times. Perhaps those who suddenly pass away are still close by, continuing to declare their love for us in the only way they can reach us, through our shared memories.

"Static Night"—Memories of living in an apartment building in Margate, New Jersey in 1990-1991. Thanks go to Harold Passman who rented me the apartment and to the many colorful neighbors I met while living there. It was there that I fought many long battles with sleep, its allies those neighbors, its weapons, feral animals, drunks, addicts and many generally unhappy people put in the way of me and a peaceful night's rest.

"Bread in the Mouths of Modern Gods and Other Dinner Party Disasters" references both the Christian concept of the body of Christ being the bread of salvation for the masses and the twisted perception of modern man toward its aging predecessors, many of whom are not accepted or respected. This brings me to "Sweeney Todd recipes" that I referenced in this poem.

I saw the 2007 version of the movie, *Sweeney Todd: The Demon Barber of Fleet Street* which starred Johnny Depp as the murderous Sweeney Todd, the vengeful main character. In the story Sweeney Todd murdered some of the upper class citizenry of London and baked portions of their bodies into meat pies, which he sold from a storefront bakery to the general public, who eagerly consumed them, finding them rather delightful, in fact. This went on for a considerable time until Sweeney Todd was found out and stopped. I liken the story to what our society is doing to its older citizenry, ignoring their needs and opinions, relegating them to utter irrelevance, grinding their accomplishments and cherished ideas into a sort of generic Communion bread for mass consumption by an uncaring, unfeeling and apathetic public who will eagerly swallow any number of baseless facts put forward in the press by dubious, perhaps nefarious sources.

Also referenced here are several notable, and notorious persons in modern history who were involved in both the introduction and institution of the failed theory of "eugenics" into the world. Sir Francis Galton, an Englishman, is to thank for eugenics, and it is ironic that the American government was the first to adopt Galton's theories on genetics as scientific fact and sought to apply his theories to its own country's social problems.

Eugenics was first introduced in 1883 by Sir Francis Galton as a theory that involved genetics in an attempt to explain why the Western white social ruling class had attained world-wide dominance, successfully colonizing the bulk of civilization as we know it. Galton made the false claim that Western Europeans were a superior race compared to the indigenous peoples of Africa, Asia, Australia, even espousing superiority over those of Slavic and Jewish decent. He made a case for the refinement and purging of modern societies, getting rid of their "feeble minded" individuals, (mainly the mentally and emotionally challenged), who might otherwise interbreed with the masses. Galton thought that their genes would eventually become dispersed among the aristocratic classes who were predominantly of Caucasian decent and had ruled the world for several centuries.

This theory became so popular among American politicians that two U.S. Presidents, Theodore Roosevelt and Woodrow Wilson, supported the concept and helped to introduce legislation that enabled the study and identification of "feeble minded" individuals in order to put a stop to them breeding. In 1910 the Eugenics Record Office opened in Long Island, New York and began collecting data that would influence the governments of California and 32 other states to adopt legislation meant to combat "feeblemindedness". Laws were passed which allowed legal, forcible incarceration and sterilization of thousands of individuals from 1909 forward until the 1947 when the U.S. Supreme Court ruled those State laws unconstitutional. These laws were selectively enforced primarily on a racially biased basis as two World Wars intervened and Americans decided that they had more important issues than the forced sterilization of Americans to consider.

In 1933 Adolf Hitler took eugenics further by introducing laws that sanctioned the round up and forced sterilization of mentally defective and congenitally stricken citizens born into German society. He quickly expanded this campaign to include those with physical deformities, and those of different ethnic origins, whom he also deemed genetically inferior, and the Jews whom Hitler and the Nazis tried to eradicate, turning Galton's "eugenics" theory into their own genocidal dogma. Thereafter, more than 400,000 German citizens were forcibly sterilized. (This paragraph and the paragraph above were referenced from the website of "Scitable", by Nature Education, www.nature.com/scitable, maintained by the Nature Publishing Group, a division of Springer Nature; Berlin, Germany, publishers of academic journals, magazines, online databases and services in science and medicine since 1869).

Of the other names cited in this poem only Charles Darwin and Gregor Mendel are acquitted of any wrongdoing, though Darwin's first cousin, Sir Francis Galton, tried to adapt and apply some of the principals Darwin had laid down in his explanations of "natural selection". Galton also attempted to explain the geo-political struggles of mankind during the previous 300 years of colonial conquests as a process of natural selection. He asserted that the white race, by virtue of its dominance of humanity, was probably genetically superior and destined to rule the planet. All of his theories have long since been debunked, but eugenics is still with us as many conspiratorialist white nationalists in America and abroad still subscribe to its false tenets.

Dr. Josef Mengele, Henry H. Goddard, Harry H. Laughlin, and J.H. Kellogg all signed on to Galton's popular beliefs and avidly promoted the "eugenics" theory to anyone who would listen to them. The various political dictators listed in this poem, Joseph Stalin of Communist Russia, Mao Tse-Tung of Communist China, Pol Pot of Cambodia, Augusto Pinochet of Chile, Mohammad Reza Pahlavi of Iran, Philippines President Ferdinand Marcos, Syria's Bashar al-Assad, Iraqi President Saddam Hussein all adopted and implemented modern methods for the extermination their political opposition. Perhaps it was time for a "eugenics" metamorphosis. Sadly, more modern forms of hate were to make their presence felt, as well. Please forgive me for leaving out any of the thousands of scoundrels similarly operating in the world today. There would not have been room in this book for them all.

About Atmosphere Press

Atmosphere Press is an independent, full-service publisher for excellent books in all genres and for all audiences. Learn more about what we do at atmospherepress.com.

We encourage you to check out some of Atmosphere's latest releases, which are available at Amazon.com and via order from your local bookstore:

How to Hypnotize a Lobster, poetry by Kristin Rose Jutras

Love is Blood, Love is Fabric, poetry by Mary De La Fuente

Lovely Dregs, poetry by Richard Sipe

Meraki, poetry by Tobi-Hope Jieun Park

Calls for Help, poetry by Greg T. Miraglia

Out of the Dark, poetry by William Guest

Lost in the Greenwood, poetry by Ellen Roberts Young

Blessed Arrangement, poetry by Larry Levy

Shadow Truths, poetry by V. Rendina

A Synonym for Home, poetry by Kimberly Jarchow

The Cry of Being Born, poetry by Carol Mariano

Big Man Small Europe, poetry by Tristan Niskanen

Lucid_Malware.zip, poetry by Dylan Sonderman

The Unordering of Days, poetry by Jessica Palmer

It's Not About You, poetry by Daniel Casey

About the Author

Jerry Lovelady is an American poet whose writing is shaped by the 1960s. A native Texan who grew up during turbulent times, his many poetic interests spring from the influential events and people of his generation. A small town boy, he saw firsthand the damage that had been done to society by segregation. The enormous disparities between whites and people of color held on longer where he grew up than in most other parts of America as State and local governments in Texas stubbornly resisted integration. Until 1968 social interaction between blacks and whites in schools, public gatherings, even normal everyday commerce was discouraged and sometimes violently prevented by the whites in power.

It was widely believed, but never proven, that in the Fall of 1968, when the black high school students in Lovelady's hometown learned that they would not be integrating into the newly built public high school that year, they burned their old school buildings to the ground rather than being forced to spend another year in their decrepit, rat infested high school. Many other events of the time shaped some of his personal values. Like many people tragedies of war and violent civil unrest caused him to question the wisdom of those who sat on the thrones of power.

The war in Vietnam was raging, Martin Luther King, Jr. was delivering his message of equality and the need for unity, university students were forming sit-ins and strikes, closing down campuses in protest of the war, as well as civil rights inequities which had gone unaddressed by the government for several generations. Tanks had rumbled down the streets of Los Angeles during the "Watts Race Riots" of August, 1965.

The Freedom Riders were making their rounds organizing protests against the Federal Government's non-enforcement of the 1947 U.S. Supreme Court's decision, *Morgan vs Virginia,* which found in favor of black patrons who rode public buses, reaffirming that segregated seating was unconstitutional.

The psychedelic generation had begun and the "Hippie" movement that Timothy Leary and others ushered in influenced young people to "...turn on, tune in, and drop out." Everything, even reality as they knew it, was suddenly open to speculation.

The poetry of T.S. Eliot and Ezra Pound, though they were from a generation half a century earlier, began to influence young people who read and popularized their works. Song writers such as Woodie Guthrie and his son Arlo Guthrie, Bob Dylan and Donovan Phillips Leitch recorded popular music in the Sixties. Their poems and song lyrics accurately depicted the state of frustration with societal norms in America and were destined to resonate with the societal revolution which was about to take place. Their words would leave an indelible mark on the generations to come after them. Somewhere along the way music became the new poetry of an American counterculture bent on change and was more popular than ever with young people the world over.

The plethora of rock and roll music makers had captured the public's attention with their messages of peaceful protest and love conquering all.

Abbie Hoffman and the Peace movement, the Weathermen, Students for a Democratic Society (SDS), The Black Panther Party all rose up to challenge the government's authority to wage war whenever it felt justified. Their protests often drew violent responses from state and local law enforcement agencies and the military.

The numerous wrongs the Federal Government had committed by the unfair treatment of blacks and the poorest members of society were being challenged with vehement disapproval. Also called into question was the indiscriminate bombing of civilians in Southeast Asia during the ongoing Vietnam War.

Worries about the escalating nuclear arms race also had most Americans on edge as two world superpowers, Russia and the United States, competed for military superiority.

In 1968 it came to light that U.S. troops were planning and carrying out military campaigns that set out to slaughter innocent civilians in Viet Nam. Reports of the infamous "My' Lai Massacre" dominated the evening news for months. More than 500 men, women and children non-combatants were executed in just one such action. Upon further investigation it was discovered and reported in the press that many more such incidents had occurred, but their public disclosures had been discouraged, or kept secret by military higher-ups, fearing that if Americans knew the truth it would harm the war effort. Upon hearing about these atrocities, young men burned their draft cards and some headed to Canada to sit out the war in shame and silence rather than be forced to take part in other unjust military operations like My' Lai.

Jerry Lovelady's poetry is fresh and personal, reflecting both what he sees as society's spiritual condition and the natural order of our world, viewed from the perspective of characters living in alternative realities. His subjects include love, life, death and aging, in some cases allegorically written, and in others simply stated with metaphors describing deep affection, longing, forgiveness, metamorphosis and joy.

Lovelady also enjoys writing poetry that focuses on our changing environment, the human condition, Nature and mankind's place in it. Sometimes his views are expressed by the living, some by imaginary or deceased individuals who may be attempting to interact with us in this worldly dimension. He invites us to explore alternative universes which we may discover are not so far removed from our own.

Human relationships and how we handle our personal problems is a favorite topic in many of Lovelady's poems, though you may detect a sardonic edge to those poems speaking directly about injustice or forced adaptation of the individual to current socially accepted norms. Whimsical fantasies, dark emotional dramas, and light-hearted verse, rhymed and otherwise, written in neo-classical style, make up the greater part of his poetry. His works stand out as a valuable addition to modern American poetic thought.

CPSIA information can be obtained
at www.ICGtesting.com
Printed in the USA
LVHW111934290922
729619LV00011B/192/J